This journal belongs to

Touch a dream to paper,

pen a soul song,

sketch the sky, trace a sigh,

write yourself strong...

This journal is a safe place where you can recall, retrace or reinvent days gone by, wonder at the mysteries before you, and simply be present. Breathe in the stunning artwork by Dora Alis, be transported to times, places and spaces, and feel the beat of other hearts as you connect to the wonder, vulnerability and honesty of innocence. Enfold yourself in warmth, love and protection as you release and explore all that you are, all that brought you to this moment, and all that you lovingly dream into being.

Enjoy!

Bewildered, I see love, I see sweetness, I see hope.
In innocence, our shared potential is laid bare.

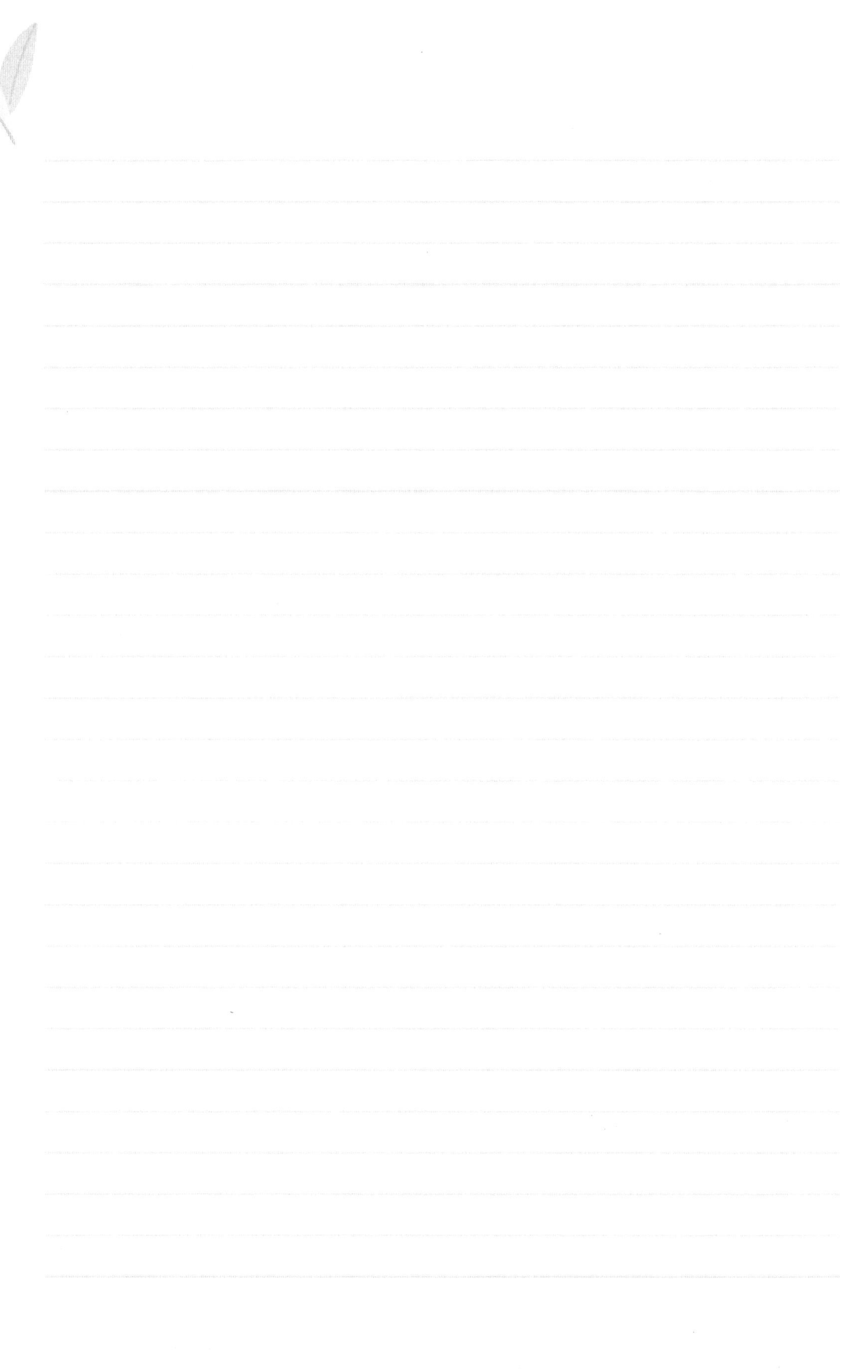

Love

A glance savoured with the calmness tenderness brings.
A moment to fall, surrender,
remember into
the magic of childhood,
with total contentment.

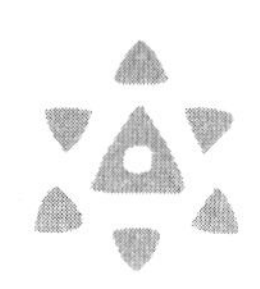

Innocence

Truth

Joy

Blessed

2009

Faithful drawing, accurate stroke,
the spell of each gesture,
its delicate care sings us from slumber
as balm of the soul,
our lost voice is reborn,
within our reach,
our hearts,
our all.

The artist finds the answer.
(I didn't know to ask the question.)

Oneness

Possibility

Not for the beauty, but for what she represents.
O, fierce and faithful mother,
O, wise and tender soul,
Shelter and strengthen,
Walk with and awaken,
the future.

Vitality

Beauty

Laughter

Knowing

Value the treasures of a naïve heart.
Nurture hope, polish grace,
cultivate love,
prosper.

You, me, we, they, no more, no less.
Grand, unassuming, perfection,
everywhere.

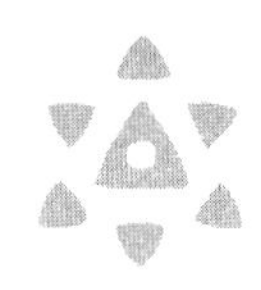

Life

Miracle

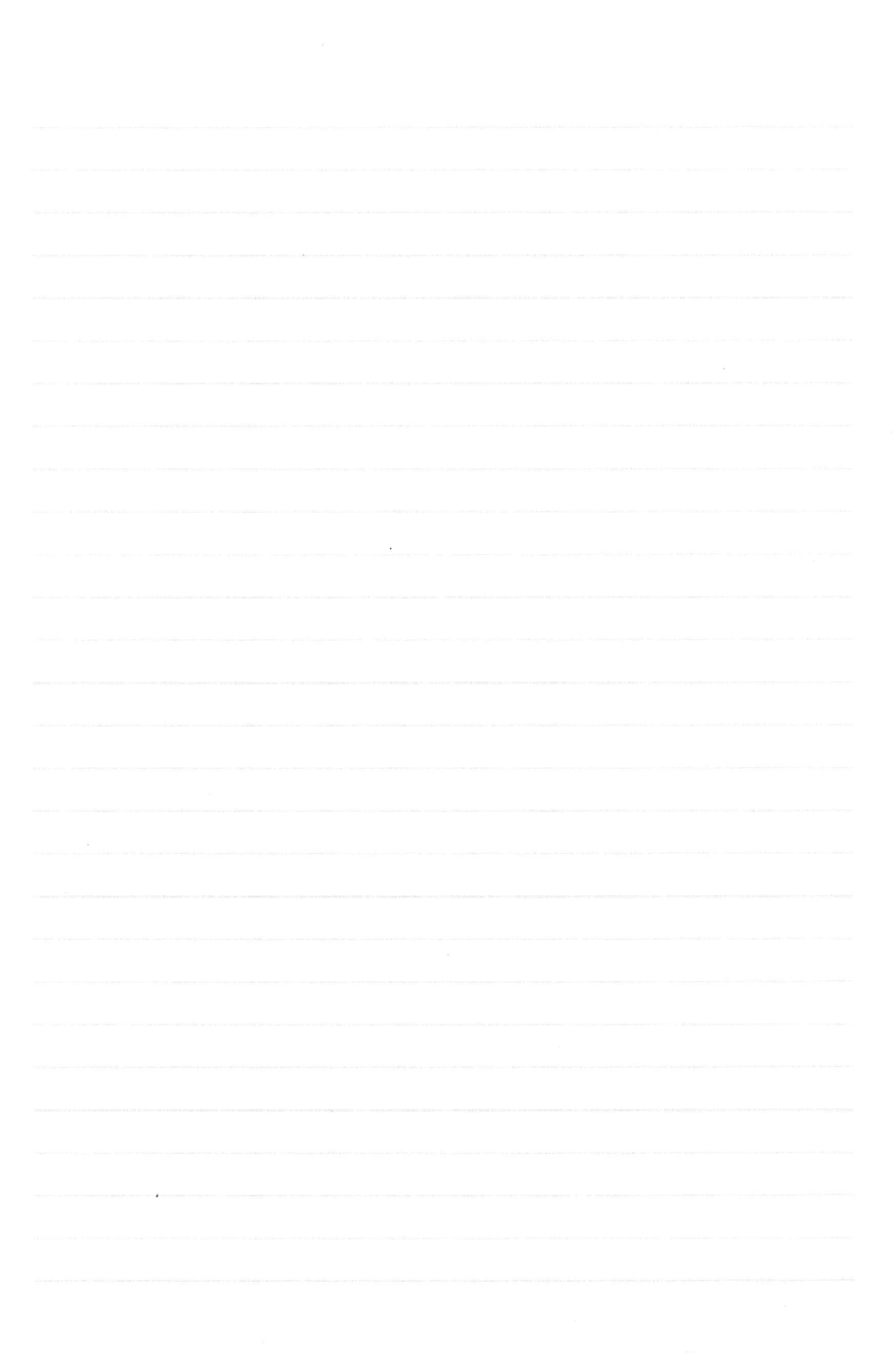

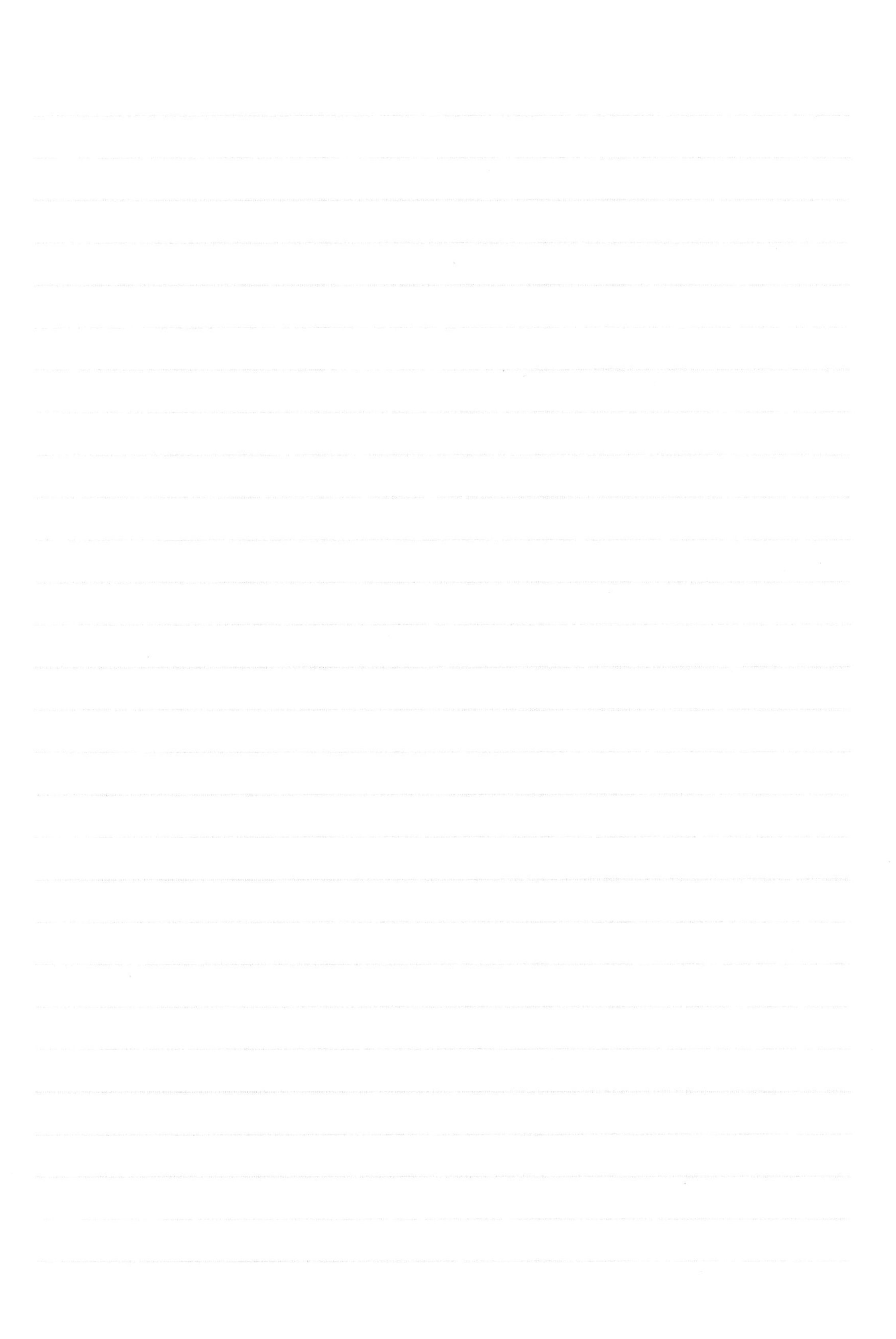

Supple with repeated kindness,
a hand reaches, a heart receives.

Dance

Imagine

Empower

Sacred

2010

There is a ductile hand that shapes it,
a restless eye that sees it,
with effort, patience, kindness,
the noble heart comes forth,
revealed.

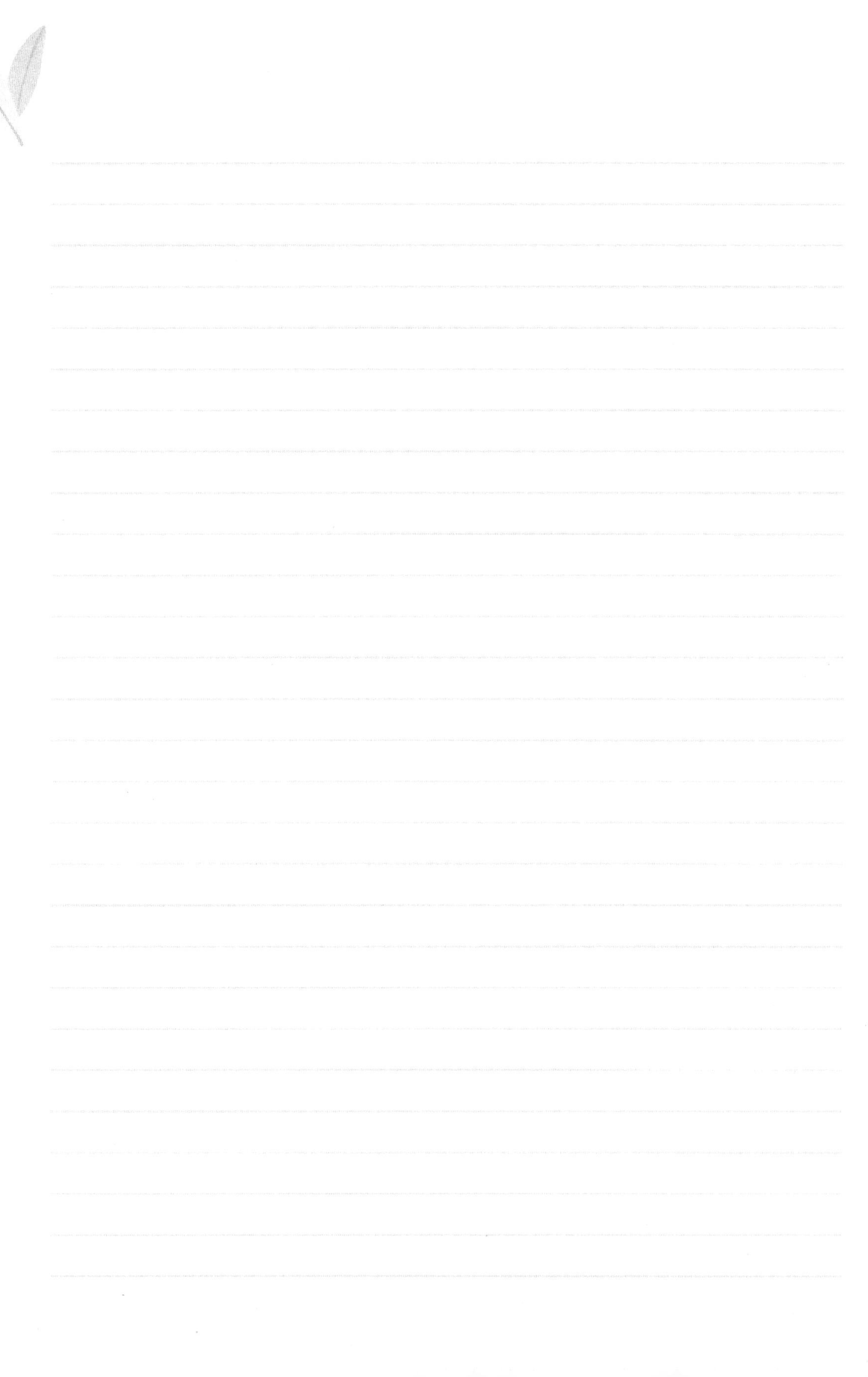

Nobility, promise, possibility,
there from the start.
Clear a way, shine a light,
Let them not lose sight
of their wonder.

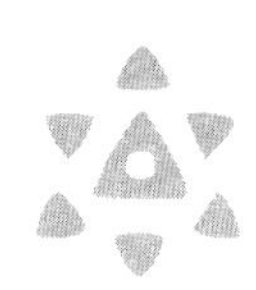

Peace

Cherish

There are many ways to love,
A road to where you once dreamed of,
There is nothing you need to remember,
Hold your head high and surrender,
Lay your soul bare and be strong.
It was here, right here, all along.

Treasure

Bountiful

Wonder

Discover

Proud

Thank you,
reminder of who I could be,
and may be again,
full of love,
complete.

Be patient child,
All I strive to remember,
you already know.

Daring

Lift your eyes in love,
Buoy your heart in hope,
You are never lost.

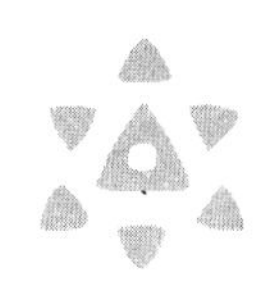

Put the keys to your imagination
in the hands of love,
steer it with care,
fuel it with hope.
Wide-eyed passenger, be taken,
to the wonder, wilderness and glory
inside us all.

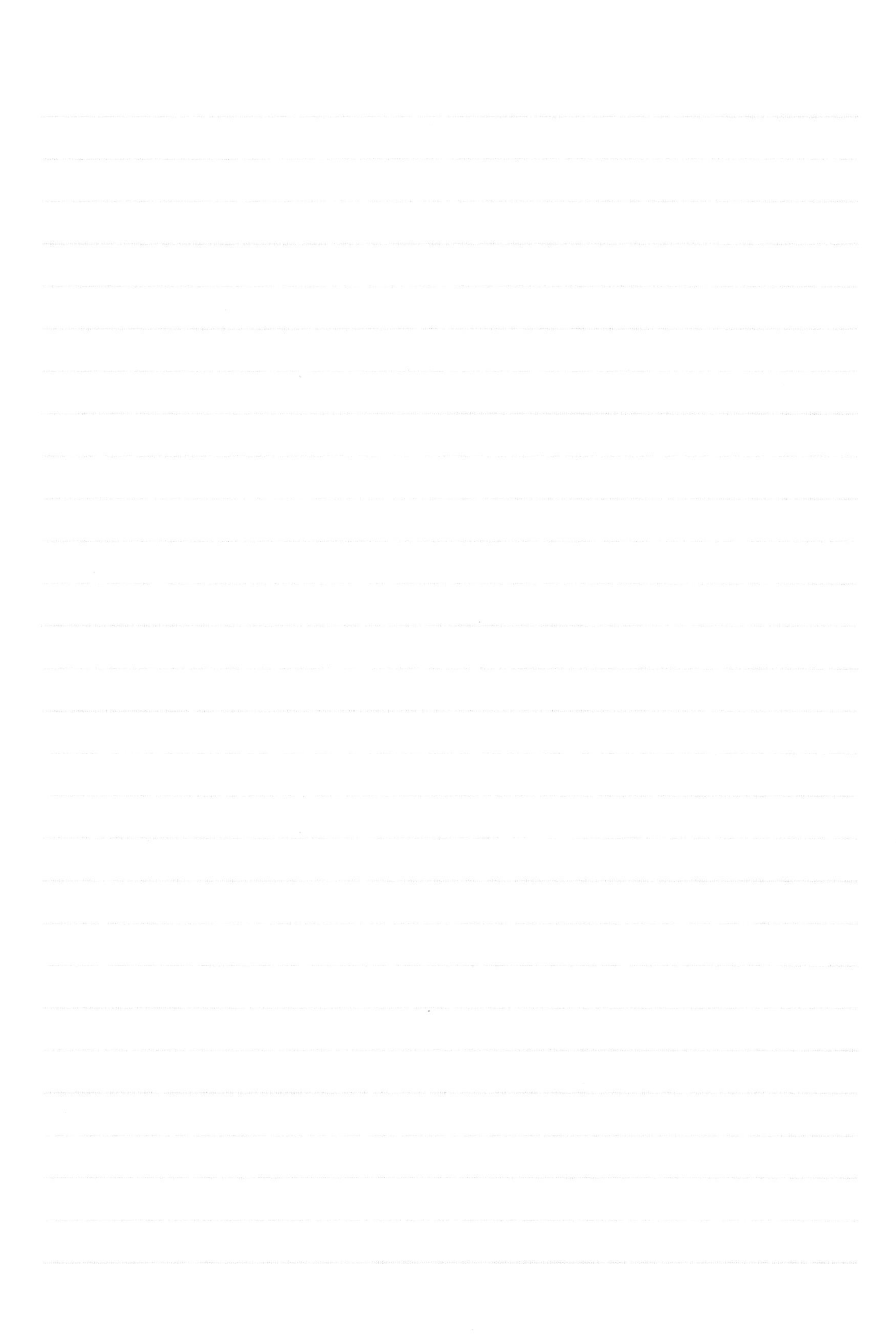

Heart

Voice

Fulfil

Blessed child, precious alchemist.
Hurt, pain and doubt, long caged and buried,
they rise in your presence,
transforming into wisdom.
I am led into gold.

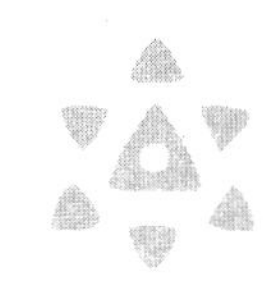

Delight!